NATURE SMARTS

WORKBOOK

AGES 4–6

From the
Environmental
Educators of
Mass Audubon

Storey Publishing

The mission of Storey Publishing is to serve our customers by publishing practical information that encourages personal independence in harmony with the environment.

Edited by Deanna F. Cook, Hannah Fries, and
    Lisa H. Hiley
Art direction and book design by Alethea Morrison
Text production by Jennifer Jepson Smith
Illustrations by © Jada Fitch

Text © 2022 by Massachusetts Audubon Society, Inc.

Storey books are available at special discounts when purchased in bulk for premiums and sales promotions as well as for fund-raising or educational use. Special editions or book excerpts can also be created to specification. For details, please call 800-827-8673, or send an email to sales@storey.com.

Storey Publishing
210 MASS MoCA Way
North Adams, MA 01247
storey.com

Printed in the United States by Lakeside Book Company
10 9 8 7 6 5 4 3 2 1

Library of Congress Cataloging-in-Publication Data on file

CONTENTS

Be Nature Smart!

Being nature smart means loving animals, plants, and their habitats. Habitats are the places where animals and plants live. Being nature smart means you want to take care of the world around you.

Use your sense of adventure to discover the world of soil, plants, birds, wildlife, and water on these pages. Then have fun exploring outdoors!

In each section, learn how you can take action to help protect animals and plants. That makes you a nature-smart Nature Hero!

The World under Your Feet

Have you ever stopped to think about the great big world under your feet? There is a lot more happening underground than the soil you see when you look down. There are rocks, bugs, worms, and more! Let us dig underground and see what we find.

Who Lives under (and in) This Log?

Soil is not just dirt. It is the top layer of earth, where plants grow and all kinds of interesting creatures live. Many of these animals make their homes or hide under logs, leaves, or rocks.

➤ Color each creature in the larger picture to match the small pictures shown below.

SALAMANDER

EARTHWORM

ANT

BEETLE

PILL BUG

MILLIPEDE

EXPLORE OUTSIDE!

Can you find any of these creatures near your home? Remember to look underneath small logs, rocks, and damp leaves.

Whose Hole Is This?

Some animals make their homes by tunneling or burrowing into the soil.

➤ Can you follow each animal to its home?

Rabbit

Groundhog

Ant

Badger

Toad

Help the Mole Find Some Lunch

Moles are soft, furry animals that live underground. They use their front feet like shovels to tunnel through the soil. Can you help this hungry mole find some yummy food?

➤ Draw one line to help the mole find some juicy worms. Draw another line to help the mole find some tasty grubs and bugs.

EXPLORE OUTSIDE!

Can you find any holes or tunnels where a small animal like a mole might live? Imagine what animals might do while they are underground!

Am I an Insect?

Did you know that all insects have a few things in common? To be an insect, you must have 3 body parts, 2 antennae, and 6 legs.

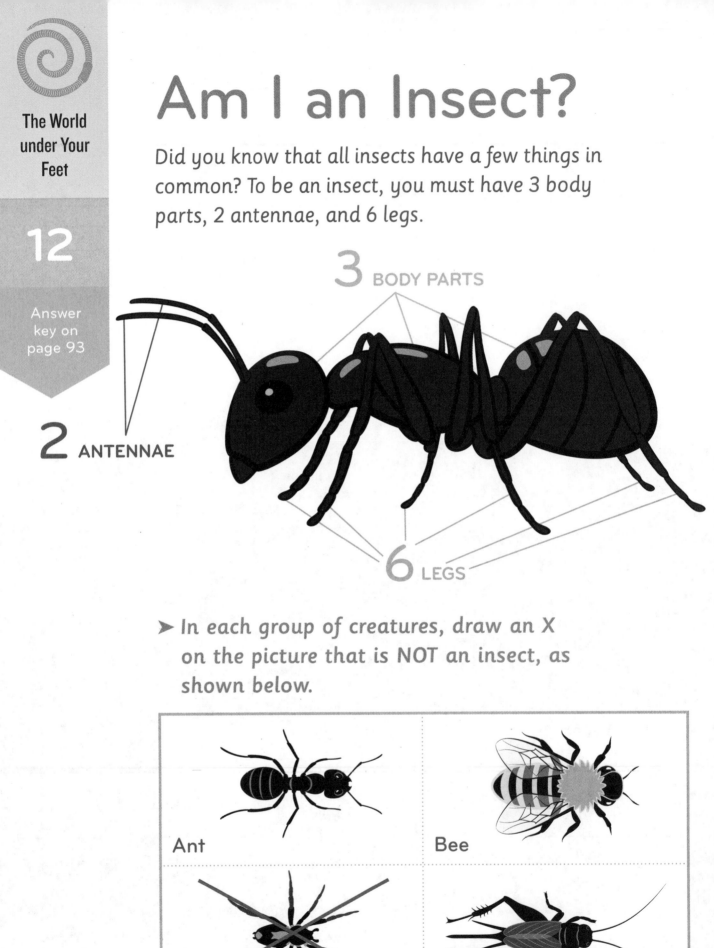

3 BODY PARTS

2 ANTENNAE

6 LEGS

➤ In each group of creatures, draw an X on the picture that is NOT an insect, as shown below.

Ant

Bee

Spider

Cricket

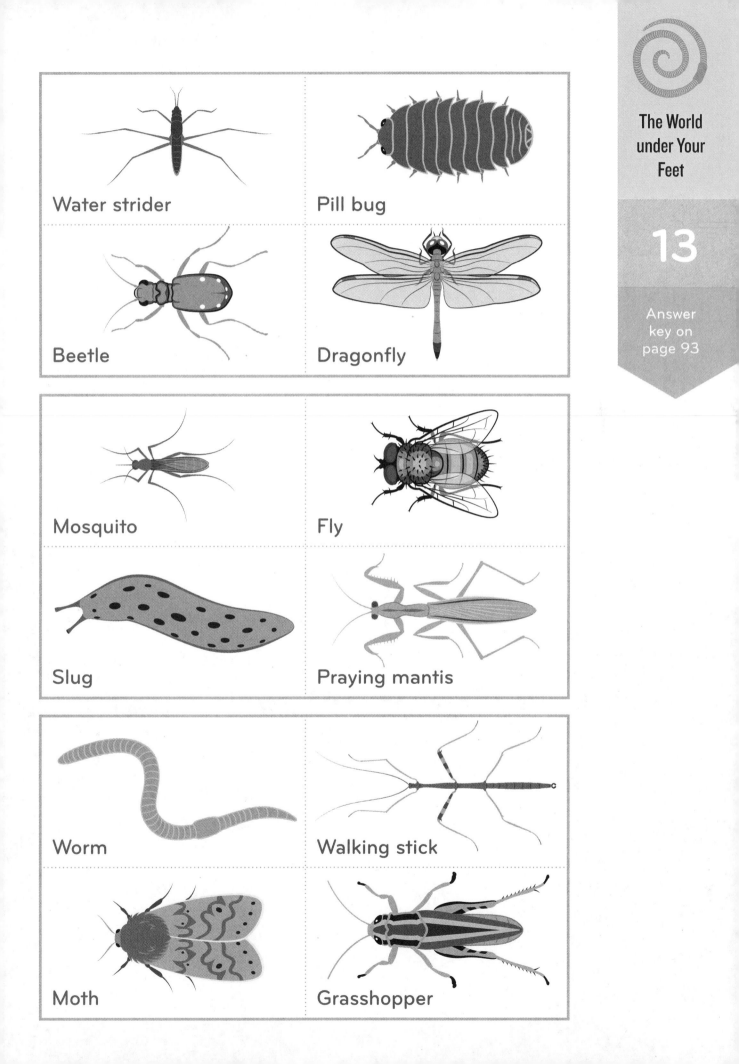

Water strider

Pill bug

Beetle

Dragonfly

Mosquito

Fly

Slug

Praying mantis

Worm

Walking stick

Moth

Grasshopper

Animal, Plant, or Mineral?

Beneath your feet is a world of animals, plants, and minerals. Minerals are nonliving things like rocks.

➤ Count how many things in the picture belong to each group. Write the number in the space.

HOW MANY ANIMALS?

HOW MANY PLANTS?

HOW MANY MINERALS?

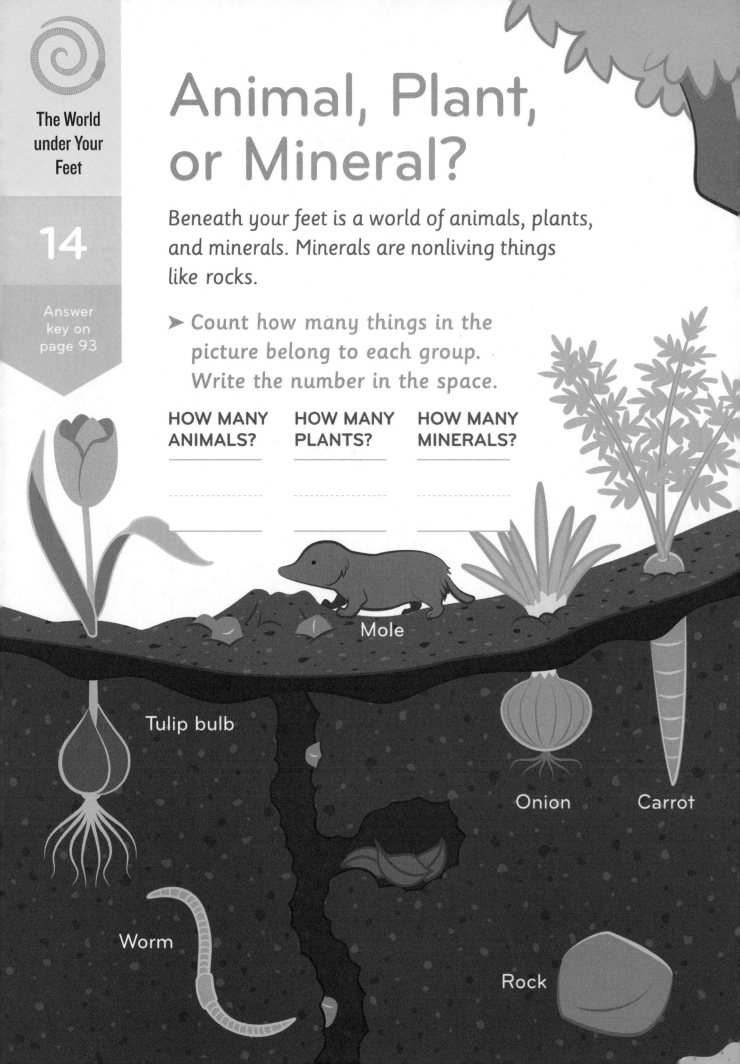

Mole

Tulip bulb

Onion

Carrot

Worm

Rock

How Many Worms Are There?

Earthworms tunnel through the dark soil. After a heavy rain, you might find lots of worms on sidewalks, grassy areas, and even in a garden. Ready, set, let's get worming!

➤ Count the worms on the sidewalk. Write the number that tells how many in all. Count the worms on the grass. Write the number that tells how many in all.

$$2 + 3 = \boxed{} \text{ in all.}$$

➤ Put a check mark next to the correct phrase.

Is the number of worms in the grass
☐ GREATER THAN,
☐ LESS THAN, or
☐ EQUAL TO
the number of worms
on the sidewalk in all?

FUN FACT
Earthworms breathe through their skin!

3 + 1 = ☐ in all.

Be a Soil Scientist

Head outside for a soil walk! Collect soil samples and make art with them. This is like making a glitter-glue picture, but it is better for our planet.

HERE IS WHAT YOU WILL NEED.

Small shovel

3 small jars or containers

Heavy paper or cardboard

Water

Glue

1 Scoop up some soil from three different places around your yard or a park. Put the soil in your jars. Try to find soil of different colors like brown, red, or gray. Try to find soil that feels different like sandy, smooth, wet, or dry.

2 When you get home, make a smudge with each kind of soil in the circles below. Rub the soil on your fingers and then rub your finger on the paper. Try adding a few drops of water to your soil to make mud. Now make a soil smudge. Does it look different when the soil is wet?

Sample 1

Sample 2

Sample 3

➤ Look at your samples.
What is the same about them?
What is different?

3 Now let's make art! Use some glue to make a simple picture or pattern on your paper or cardboard. Sprinkle dry soil over the glue. When the glue dries, brush off the extra soil and enjoy your artwork!

Soil Scavenger Hunt

☐ Smooth rock

☐ Bumpy rock

☐ Tiny rock

☐ Worm

☐ Pill bug

☐ Mushroom

➤ Head outside for a scavenger hunt! See how many of these things you can find on the ground.

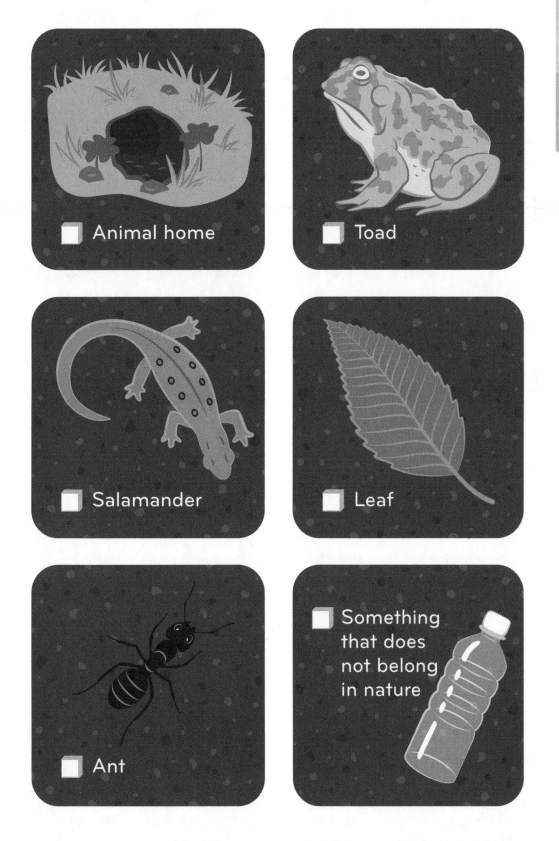

☐ Animal home

☐ Toad

☐ Salamander

☐ Leaf

☐ Ant

☐ Something that does not belong in nature

Make a Coverboard Habitat!

A coverboard is a flat wooden board placed on the forest floor or in a garden or backyard. Salamanders, worms, pill bugs, and other creatures can use coverboards for a moist shelter just as they might use leaves or logs.

★ All you need are some pieces of untreated wood about 1 foot square. Place the boards in a line 2 to 3 feet apart.

★ After a few days, peek underneath to see if any creatures found your habitat. Draw a picture of what you find.

★ Go back and check on another day. Do you see the same or different creatures? Do you find more creatures on a rainy day or a sunny day?

Fur, Scales, and Tails

Birds, mammals, amphibians, and reptiles may be closer than you think. They might live in a nearby park or even your backyard. Look for clues, but always give wild animals lots of space. They are shy and may protect themselves if they feel afraid.

Whose Tracks Are These?

Have you ever seen footprints in the snow or mud, then wondered who made them? When animals walk on soft ground, they leave their footprints behind. Every animal leaves a different kind of track. People can learn a lot from looking at animal tracks.

➤ Follow the lines to match each animal to its tracks.

Robin

Tortoise

Fox

Sidewinder snake

Bison

BE A SCIENTIST
Make a Track Box

Who are your wild animal neighbors? Make a track box and see who comes to visit!

Soil

Water

Tracking guide

Squirrel

Mouse

Large cookie sheet (or thick piece of cardboard)

$\frac{1}{4}$ cup cut-up vegetables and fruits

Dog

Cat

Raccoon

Bird

1 Find a good spot for setting up your track box. Think about what places animals might visit. Some places may be next to a deck or stairs, by a bush, or near a body of water.

2 Mix soil and water to make mud. Add water a little at a time so the mud does not get too wet. Make the mud thick so that it holds the shape of a track. Test it by making a handprint.

3 Spread the mud out on a flat tray or piece of cardboard, or put the mud directly on the ground.

4 Leave a few pieces of food in the middle of the mud to attract animals.

5 Check your track box daily. Add water if the mud gets dry. If you see any tracks, draw a picture of what you see.

Animal Adaptations

Animals protect themselves from predators (other animals that might eat them) in very different ways. Some animals have armor or spines, some use bad smells or poison, and some are really good at hiding. All these ways that animals stay safe are called *adaptations*.

➤ Draw lines to match each animal to its adaptation.

Turtle

Porcupine

Skunk

EXPLORE OUTSIDE!

Can you find an
animal in your
neighborhood that
uses an adaptation
to protect itself and
stay safe?

Toad

Copperhead

Bird

Help the Turtle Get to the Pond

This turtle has found a safe spot to dig her nest and lay her eggs. Now she wants to go back to the pond where she lives.

➤ Help the turtle find the right path back to the pond.

Find My Tail!

Each of these animals uses a tail for a different purpose.

➤ Draw lines to match each animal to its tail.

BEAVER
"I slap my big, flat tail on the water to give an alarm."

RATTLESNAKE
"I rattle my tail to warn others to stay away."

BLUE JAY
"I use my tail to steer and balance while I fly."

POSSUM
"I use my naked tail to help me climb trees."

SNAPPING TURTLE
"I have spikes on my tail to protect me from predators."

FOX
"My bushy tail helps me stay warm in winter."

Happy Habitat

Every living thing has a habitat. A habitat has everything an animal needs—food, water, and a place to stay safe.

OCEAN HABITAT

Dolphin

Sea turtle

Octopus

Frog

FOREST HABITAT

Deer

Penguin

Black bear

Woodpecker

➤ In each group of creatures, draw an X on the animal that does not belong in that habitat, as shown in the first box.

POND HABITAT

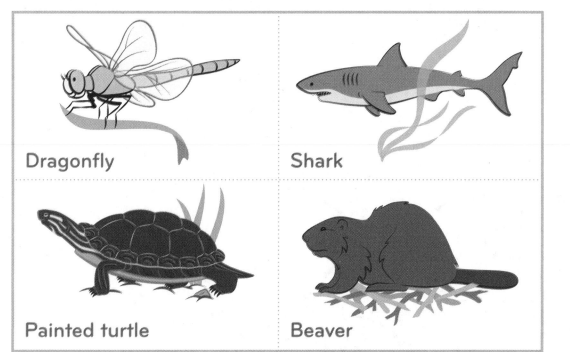

Dragonfly

Shark

Painted turtle

Beaver

DESERT HABITAT

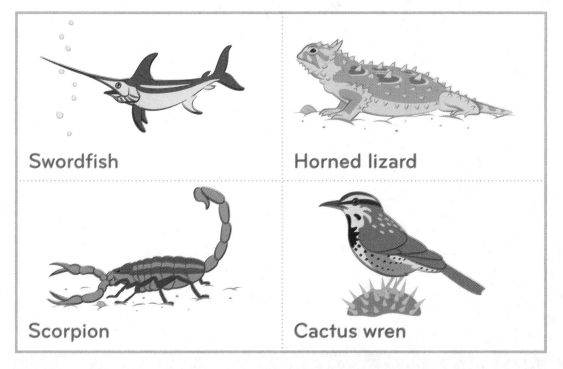

Swordfish

Horned lizard

Scorpion

Cactus wren

Animal Homes

Animals make their homes in habitats. They might build dens, nests, or other cozy places to raise their babies and keep them safe.

➤ Connect the dots to discover what animal makes its home in this rocky stream.

➤ Connect the dots to discover what animal makes its home in this desert cactus.

Answer key on page 94

At Home in the Beaver Pond

When beavers build dams in rivers and streams, they create a new habitat called a *pond*. The beaver builds a home called a *lodge*. Many other kinds of animals also make their homes at the pond.

➤ In the beaver pond picture, draw a circle around each animal whose name is given below.

RACCOON

MOOSE

BEAVER

RED-WINGED BLACKBIRD

CRAYFISH

DRAGONFLY

TADPOLE

GREAT BLUE HERON

TURTLE

FROG

FUN FACT
Frogs do not need to drink water because they absorb it through their skin.

CREATE
A Beaver Dam

Beavers are great engineers! They respond to the sound of rushing water by building a dam to slow the flow of the water.

➤ Use your engineering skills like a beaver to dam up a flow of water.

HERE IS WHAT YOU WILL NEED.

Modeling clay or thick mud

Stones

Sticks

Moss

Bark

A wide, flat-bottomed container with high sides

Water source (hose or watering can)

FUN FACT
A beaver's teeth never stop growing! But beavers are always wearing their teeth down by gnawing on wood, so their teeth do not get too long.

1 Spread a layer of modeling clay or mud across the bottom of your container.

2 Build up your dam by placing the stones on the bottom, and then adding sticks, moss, and bark. Break bigger sticks to make smaller ones, just like a beaver would do!

3 Pour water into one side of your container. Does your dam hold back the water? See if you can turn one side of your container into a pond.

4 Ask yourself, What materials worked best? What happened when you tried to stop the water?

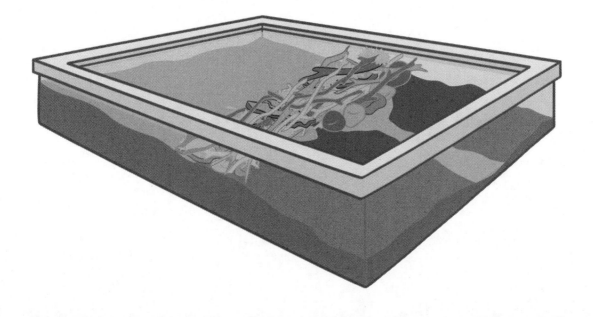

Animal Scavenger Hunt

☐ Feather or piece of fur

☐ Sound from an animal

☐ Place where a bird might live

☐ Place where a mammal might live

☐ Track

☐ Insect

Animals are all around us. They leave clues behind.

➤ Go outside for a walk. See how many animals or clues you can find.

☐ Bird

☐ Reptile

☐ Four-legged mammal

☐ Two-legged mammal

Did you know that humans are mammals?

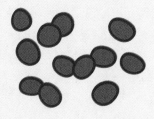

☐ Animal scat (poop)

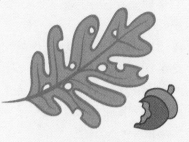

☐ Something that has been chewed

BE A NATURE HERO

Help Turtles, Frogs, and Salamanders Cross the Road

During the spring, turtles, frogs, and salamanders head to ponds and other wet places to lay their eggs. Often they have to cross busy roads. You can be a Nature Hero by helping them get to their egg-laying spots safely. Here are some tips.

★ Be careful when riding your bike or scooter. Watch where you are going—there might be a turtle in the path!

★ If you see a turtle crossing the road, tell a grown-up. They can help you either by stopping traffic (if it is safe) or by helping the turtle cross the road. Always move the turtle in the direction it is already going.

★ Learn about frog and salamander crossings. Join a local nature group to learn about these animals' spring migration.

NOTE: Only grown-ups should touch wild turtles. They should always wash their hands afterward because reptiles can carry bacteria called salmonella.
   Also, never pick up a snapping turtle by hand. Use a shovel to direct it across the road safely.

Feathered Friends

Birds of a feather flock together. And all birds have feathers! Birds are easy to find with our eyes and ears, and are often easy to observe. Look for birds in the air, on the ground, and in the water. You can find them just about anywhere!

Bird Sizes

Birds come in many different sizes, from tiny hummingbirds to soaring eagles.

➤ Write the numbers 1 to 5 to put the birds in order from smallest to biggest.

1

Hummingbird

Bald eagle

Turkey

Puffin

Swallow

CREATE
Bird Tracks

Have you ever seen bird tracks in the sand, mud, or snow? You can make your own bird tracks with a few simple items!

HERE IS WHAT YOU WILL NEED.

Construction paper

Pipe cleaners

Paint

1 Most birds have four toes: three in front and one in the back! Twist pipe cleaners to look like the feet of birds:

2 Dip your bird feet in paint and walk them across the paper.

FUN FACT
Some birds can move one of their toes from the front to the back of their foot. This makes an X shape that is better for gripping things.

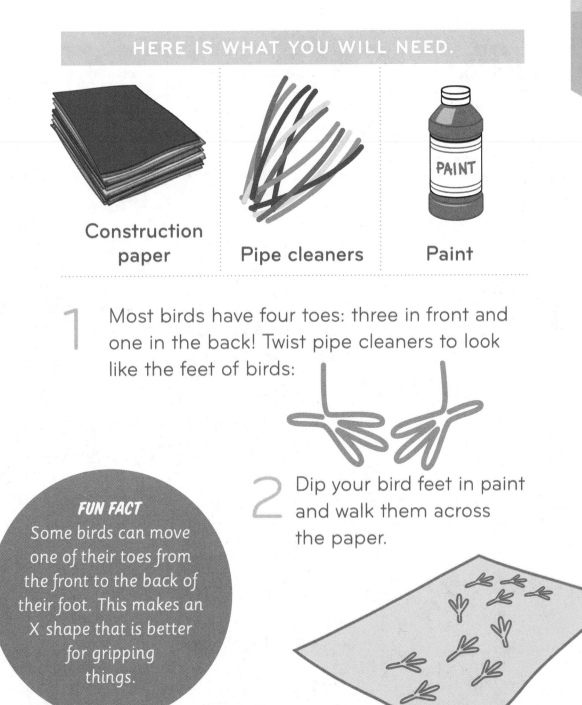

Help the Bird Feed the Babies

Nests protect baby birds until they learn to fly and find their own food. This robin has found a worm to feed to his babies. Can you help him get back to his nest?

◄ Start here ►

EXPLORE OUTSIDE!

Go for a bird walk.
Listen for different
bird sounds. Can
you make sounds
like a bird?

Are the birdsongs
short, long, loud,
or soft? Do birds
squeak, squawk,
or squeal? Can you
see the bird making
the sound? How
many different bird
calls can you hear?

Nest Rhymes

Birds build their nests in all kinds of different places!

➤ Fill in the last word of each rhyme to learn something about these birds and their nests.

Ducks hide their nests so they can't be found.

They're not up high— they're on the

G_____ _____ .

A woodpecker nest is hard to see.

It's hidden away in a hollow

T_____ _____ .

An osprey's nest almost touches the sky.

It's built on a pole, way up

H___ ___ ___.

A hummingbird is quick and shiny.

It's the smallest bird, so its nest is

T___ ___ ___.

Building nests of mud that are safe from harm,

Barn swallows are found on many a

F___ ___ ___.

CREATE

A Seedy Treat Bird Feeder

Birds who love seeds will flock to this tasty little bird feeder. Try making several of them and hanging them in different places. Who came to visit your feeder? How long did it take before all the birdseed disappeared?

HERE IS WHAT YOU WILL NEED.

String or yarn

A pinecone or toilet paper tube

Vegetable shortening, smooth peanut butter, or sunflower seed butter

Birdseed

1 Tie a piece of string or yarn around the pinecone or toilet paper tube.

2 Spread the shortening, peanut butter, or sunflower seed butter all over the bird feeder.

3 Sprinkle birdseed all over the bird feeder until it is covered. You may need to lightly push the birdseed in so it sticks.

4 Hang your bird feeder in a place where you can easily observe it. Tie it high enough so the birds will be safe from predators.

How Many Birds?

Many kinds of birds migrate every year. They might fly north to find good nesting habitat in the spring and south to find more food in the winter. Birds of the same kind often migrate together in groups.

➤ Count the birds in each group. Add or subtract, then write the answer.

This flock of geese had 7 birds, and then 4 more birds came to join them. How many geese are there now?

$7 + 4 = \underline{\hspace{2cm}}$ now.

There were 15 in this flock of warblers, but 2 lost their way. How many warblers are left?

$15 - 2 = \underline{\hspace{2cm}}$ left.

A group of 6 whooping cranes touched down in Texas, and then 6 more joined them. How many whooping cranes are there now?

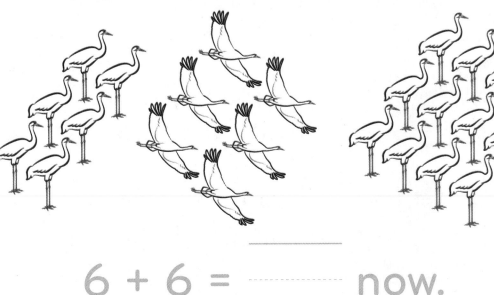

6 + 6 = _____ now.

There were 7 wood ducks swimming in the pond, and then 2 flew away. How many ducks are still left swimming?

7 − 2 = _____ left.

Bird Scavenger Hunt

☐ Feather

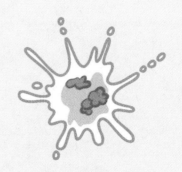

☐ Bird droppings

☐ Bird on a branch

☐ Sound of a bird call

☐ Bird nest

☐ Bird flying

➤ *See how many of these birds or signs of birds you can find in your neighborhood.*

☐ Crow

☐ Robin

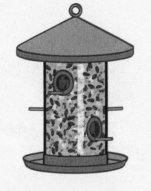

☐ Bird feeder

☐ Bird in the water

☐ Woodpecker hole

☐ Bird eating something

BE A NATURE HERO

Join a Bird Count!

Every year thousands of people take part in bird counts with groups like the National Audubon Society or the Cornell Lab of Ornithology. (Visit their websites for details.) The information collected helps scientists with their research. Being part of a bird count is fun!

★ Pick a spot outdoors, like a park or your backyard.

★ Spend 10 minutes listening and observing.

★ Make a list of the different birds you see and how many of each kind.

★ To share what you observe with a scientist, ask an adult to help you enter your information online.

BLUE JAY

MOURNING DOVE

Of course, you can listen and look for birds at any time without keeping a list. Here are pictures of some birds you might see.

ROBIN

CARDINAL

BLACK-CAPPED CHICKADEE

Plant Power

Plants are all around us and range from the very small to the incredibly tall! When you go outside, look around. How many different colors, shapes, and sizes of plants can you see?

What Grows from These Seeds?

Most plants grow from seeds.

➤ Can you follow the lines from the seeds to the plants they come from?

60

Answer
key on
page 95

Pine

Sunflower

Oak

Dandelion

Corn

Maple

Answer key on page 95

EXPLORE OUTSIDE!

Go on a seed hunt. Can you find any seeds near where you live? Do you know what kind of plant they will grow into?

You can look around your kitchen for seeds, too. (Hint: Do you ever make popcorn?)

A Seed Catches a Ride

Some seeds use animals to catch a ride! When an animal eats a berry, it carries the seeds in its belly until it poops. Other seeds, like burs, stick to the fur of animals (or your socks!) to hitch a ride.

Start here

➤ Starting at the prickly bush by the green house, trace the dotted line to see how this dog gave some burs a ride!

STOP

From Seed to Flower

How does a seed grow into a plant?

➤ Number the pictures in order from 1 to 5 to show how a tiny seed becomes a big, beautiful sunflower.

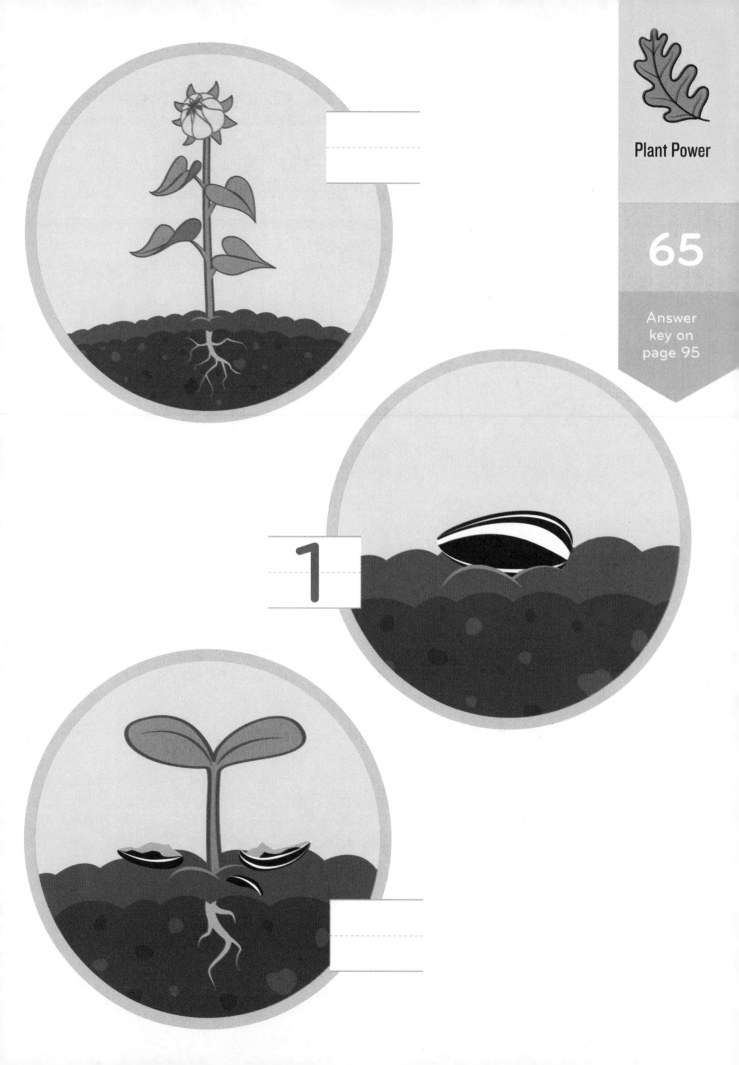

1

Window Sprouts

No place to grow a garden? No problem! You can watch seeds sprout in any sunny window.

HERE IS WHAT YOU WILL NEED.

Paper towels

Water

Tape

Plastic bag
(sandwich-size will do)

3–4 seeds, preferably
different kinds

1 Look through your yard, pantry, and refrigerator to find some seeds. Beans (uncooked), popcorn kernels, and fruit and vegetable seeds all work!

2 Place a folded paper towel and the seeds in the plastic bag.

3 Pour just enough water into the bag to make the paper towel wet but not have a puddle in the bottom of the bag.

4 Close the bag and tape it to a window that gets lots of sun.

5 Check your experiment daily. What is happening?

Leaves or Needles

Trees are either deciduous (dih-SID-joo-us) or coniferous (kuh-NIH-fur-us). Deciduous trees grow leaves in the spring and lose them in the fall. Some trees also grow flowers that become fruit.

➤ Color the flowers pink. Color the apples red. Count how many of each and write the number.

APPLE TREE

How many flowers are there? _____

How many apples are there? _____

Coniferous trees have needles instead of leaves. The needles stay green all year long, even when it snows. A coniferous tree also has cones. Inside the cones are the seeds.

➤ Color the cones brown. Color the snowflakes blue. Count how many of each and write the number.

PINE TREE

How many cones are there? _____

How many snowflakes are there? _____

Plant Power

70

BE A SCIENTIST
Observe a Tree

Find a special tree near your home. It should be one that really catches your eye! Try to visit your tree often. What does your tree look like?

➤ Draw a picture of your special tree.

➤ Write down what you like about your tree.

_____

_____

_____

_____

_____

➤ **Every time you visit your tree, take photos, make notes, or draw pictures.**

Notice how it changes from day to day, month to month, or season to season. You can use your photos, pictures, and notes to make a book all about your special tree.

FUN FACT
Some kinds of trees grow to be more than 100 feet tall. That's as tall as 3 or 4 houses stacked on top of each other!

CREATE
Leaf Creatures

In the autumn, leaves of every shape, size, and color fall to the ground. You can use them to make pictures of animals!

HERE IS WHAT YOU WILL NEED.

Leaves of different shapes, sizes, and colors

Construction paper

Glue

Scissors

1 Collect leaves of as many different shapes, sizes, and colors as you can find.

2 Arrange your leaves on construction paper to make your very own leaf creatures. Use glue to stick them to the paper.

3 You can cut out eyes or use googly eyes!

Plant Bingo

➤ Look for these objects outside. When you find one, draw an X through it. The center square is for any tree-related item you see. Three in a row wins!

TREE BINGO

	FREE SPACE	

➤ Look for these objects both inside and outside your home. When you find one, draw an X through it. The center square is for any seed-related item you see. Three in a row wins!

SEED BINGO

FREE SPACE

Plant Power

76

Plant Flowers for Wildlife

Bring some flowering plants to your home or neighborhood! Visit a local nursery to find out about native plants that grow well in your area.

You can grow your plants from seeds, or start with seedlings. Use a window box, a small pot, or a raised garden bed. Insects will visit the flowers to collect pollen, birds will snack on the seeds, and a toad may use the container for shelter.

Here are a few common plants that support wildlife.

★ Asters

★ Cardinal flowers

★ Common milkweed

★ Bee balm

★ Purple coneflower

★ Great blue lobelia

★ Salvia

PURPLE
CONEFLOWER

BEE BALM

ASTERS

Weather, Water, and Wind

Weather is all around us. It determines what we wear and the kinds of things we do outside. Grab your sense of adventure and head outdoors to be a weather watcher! (Look out a window first to see if you need to wear a coat and hat!)

Where Does the Water Go?

There is water all around us. When rain falls from the clouds, where does it go? Sometimes it falls in rivers, lakes, the ocean, or a puddle. Water can even land in your garden or fall in your glass of lemonade.

➤ Follow each raindrop to see where it ends up!

FUN FACT

Most raindrops are smaller than ¼ inch. Look at the ruler to see how big that is. How big do they look to you when they are falling from the sky?

BE A SCIENTIST
Will It Get Wet?

Have you ever noticed how raindrops make little beads on your raincoat or boots? When a raindrop hits the soil or the sidewalk, does it do the same thing? What does water do when it hits your skin? Test what water does when you drop it on different materials.

HERE IS WHAT YOU WILL NEED.

Spray bottle or eyedropper

Water

Different materials—paper towels, tin foil, wax paper, note paper, metal tray, glass or ceramic dish, dish towel

1   Slowly spray or drip water onto a few different materials and observe what happens. What does the water do on the different materials?

2   Next, take your water outside and test it on natural materials such as dirt, sand, leaves, and bark. Did you notice any differences?

Every Snowflake Is Special

Did you know that every snowflake that falls from a cloud is one of a kind? That means no two snowflakes are alike!

➤ In each row, draw a circle around the one snowflake that does not match the others.

Cloud Match

Look up in the sky! Have you noticed that there are many kinds of clouds? Different clouds have different names. Here are some common ones to look for.

CIRRUS
thin, wispy clouds

CUMULUS
puffy cottonball clouds

STRATUS
thick, blanketlike
clouds

NIMBUS
dark rain or snow clouds
and thunderheads

➤ Find the matching clouds. Draw a line to show which clouds are the same.

EXPLORE OUTSIDE!

Head outside and look up! Are there any clouds in the sky? Try lying on the ground to get a better look.

Are they puffy? Wispy? Dark? Flat? Can you guess whether it will rain today?

CREATE
Sun Prints

The sun's light is so powerful that it can cause colors to fade from things like paper and fabric. Test the power of the sun by making your own sun prints.

HERE IS WHAT YOU WILL NEED.

Colored construction paper

Natural objects

1 On a bright sunny morning, gather a few pieces of colored paper and take them outside.

2 Collect a few objects from nature that will fit on the paper, such as leaves, shells, rocks, and sticks. Look for different interesting shapes.

FUN FACT

It takes 8 minutes for light from the sun to reach the earth. Try setting a timer for 8 minutes. Imagine light leaving the sun. When the timer goes off, the light that left the sun is now shining on the earth!

3 Place your paper in a sunny place and arrange one or more objects on top of each sheet. You may need to tape some objects down if it is windy.

4 Leave the construction paper outside in the sun for the rest of the day. When you remove the objects, you should see a dark print where the object blocked the light of the sun!

What Do You Wear When . . .

The weather affects all sorts of things in our lives, from what activities we do to what clothes we wear.

➤ Choose the clothes that you would wear for each kind of weather. Draw a circle on the correct picture in each box.

When the weather is hot and sunny, I go to the beach in my

After it rains, I put on my

and jump in the puddles.

When a cold wind blows, I wear my

When it snows, I like to put my

on my hands and build a snowman.

I always put a

on my snowman to keep his neck warm!

Staying Warm

In the winter, animals have different ways to stay warm and move around in the deep snow.

➤ Trace over the letters of each animal's name. When you're done, say the name out loud.

FOX listens and pounces into the snow to catch a mouse.

CHIPMUNK
sleeps underground.

MOUSE
makes tunnels under the snow to hide from the fox.

CARDINAL
fluffs up all its feathers.

SNAKE
curls up inside a
rock wall.

SQUIRREL
snuggles down in a
hollow tree.

Woolly Bear
CATERPILLAR
burrows into dead
leaves under the snow.

TOAD
goes into a deep sleep
underground near the
base of a tree.

CREATE
A Windsock

While we cannot see the wind, we can feel it when it blows! We can also observe how it moves the things around us. Go outside. Is there any wind blowing now? How do you know? Make a windsock to help you see how strong the wind is and tell what direction it is blowing.

HERE IS WHAT YOU WILL NEED.

Coloring materials (such as markers or crayons)

Heavy paper (such as construction paper or cardstock)

Glue or tape

Tissue paper, yarn, or ribbon

Hole punch

String or yarn

1 Decorate 1 sheet of paper. Roll the paper into a tube with the design on the outside. Glue or tape the edge of the paper to hold it together.

2 Cut the tissue paper into streamers or use lengths of ribbon or yarn. Glue or tape the streamer ends to the inside of one end of the paper tube.

3 On the other end of the tube, punch 2 holes and tie a loop of string through them.

4 Hang the windsock outside so that when the wind blows, it will fly.

5 Check on your windsock once a day. Is it flying high or low? What directions are the ribbons flying?

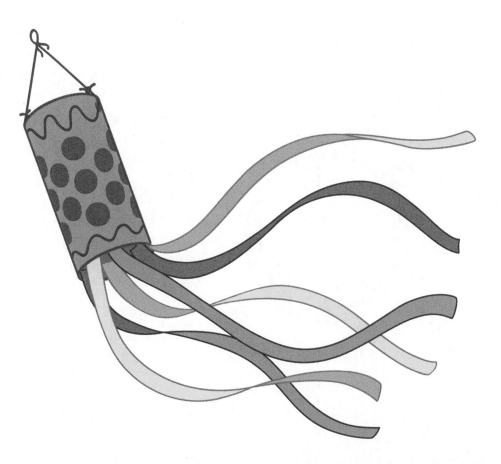

BE A NATURE HERO

Use Water Wisely

It might seem like there is plenty of water in the world. You just turn on the faucet and it comes out. After you use the water, it disappears down the drain. But in some places, rivers run dry because there is not enough water.

Water is important! How can you save water and make better use of the clean water you have? Here are some Nature Hero tips.

★ Remind your family to run the dishwasher and washing machine with full loads.

★ Can you take a shower in under 5 minutes? Set up a timer!

★ Turn off the water while you are brushing your teeth, rather than let it run the whole time.

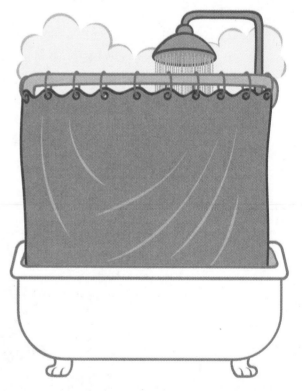

Answer Key

PAGES 8–9

PAGES 14–15

HOW MANY
ANIMALS?

4

HOW MANY
PLANTS?

4

HOW MANY
MINERALS?

4

PAGES 16–17

2 + 3 = 5

3 + 1 = 4

Less than

PAGES 10–11

PAGES 24–25

PAGE 13

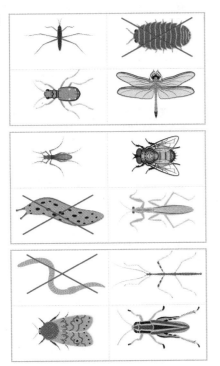

PAGES 28–29

PAGES 30–31

PAGES 36–37

PAGES 32–33

PAGES 38–39

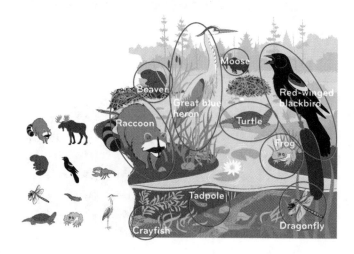

Moose

Beaver

Great blue
heron

Red-winged
blackbird

Raccoon

Turtle

Frog

Tadpole

Crayfish

Dragonfly

PAGES 34–35

PAGE 46

1 Hummingbird

Bald
eagle 5

4 Turkey

3 Puffin

2 Swallow

PAGES 48–49

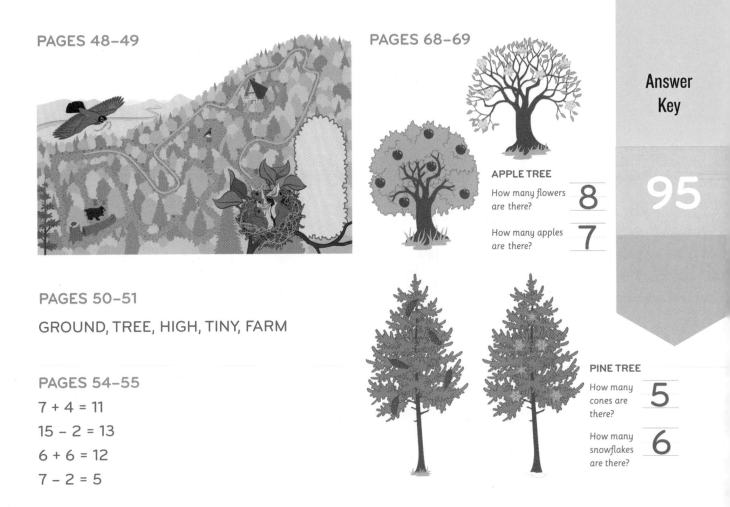

PAGES 68–69

APPLE TREE

How many flowers are there? **8**

How many apples are there? **7**

PINE TREE

How many cones are there? **5**

How many snowflakes are there? **6**

PAGES 50–51

GROUND, TREE, HIGH, TINY, FARM

PAGES 54–55

7 + 4 = 11

15 – 2 = 13

6 + 6 = 12

7 – 2 = 5

PAGES 60–61

PAGES 64–65

PAGES 78–79

PAGE 81

PAGES 86–87

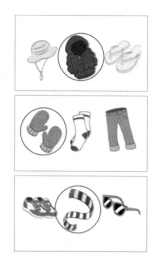

PAGE 83